Which Walks

LAURA MORIARTY

Which Walks

NIGHTBOAT BOOKS

NEW YORK

ISBN: 978-1-643-62277-4

Cover art : *which walk* by Laura Moriarty, 2022
Design and composition by Kit Schluter
Typeset in EB Garamond

Cataloging-in-publication data is available
from the Library of Congress

Nightboat Books
New York
www.nightboat.org

"we walk continually// on thin air"

—H.D., *The Walls Do Not Fall*

TABLE OF CONTENTS

PROLOGUE

AN OLD WOMAN WANDERS the pestilential streets. She sees herself from the outside. She feels like an archeologist of the present. She makes "finds." At first, she is afraid to pick up the items in case they are covered in viruses. Eventually she lets go of that idea and many objects appear on her worktable. Some are arranged into boxes. She finds herself to be obsessed with metal, glass, game pieces, marbles, tools, jewelry, and figurines, and with assembling.

The days come together in the form of these objects and their arranging. The woman's incessant movement is simultaneously search and research. Gradually the collected items (as with the words and notes collected from each morning's reading) are assembled. The practice of assembling morphs to one of attaching and building. At a local beach, once a dynamite factory, she discovers a source of sea glass and later, in a nearby town, one of stained-glass remnants. She attaches them to a metal grid with aluminum wire. In a lucky break, she has her first art exhibition of this and other works. She writes in relation to the making and walking—assembling a series of linked pieces called Which Walks. This is where the love comes in.

The old woman is in love with the bits she collects and with the people in the street and in the world. Afraid for their mutual futures and her own, she worries also for their presents. She hears guns at night and reads about them in the day. She agrees with the chalked signs on the street claiming "we are in this together." She zooms, and occasionally walks, with close friends and family. They keep each other alive. She continues to work.

All of it—walking, writing, assembling, time— seems like a single practice involving lines. Eventually, drawing is added to assembling. The lines of what she now sees is a long poem are written in relation to her art practice, to her own precarity, and to that of her loved ones, which, terrifyingly, seems to include everyone. She rereads the long poems of her youth by H.D., Williams, and Zukofsky, also rereading Duncan, Brathwaite, Howe, Dahlen, DuPlessis, M. NourbeSe Philip. She gets all the way through Nate Mackey's *Double Trio* and then starts back in at the beginning. She feels at the beginning of something herself, though she has just turned seventy.

An inveterate Blakean, she rereads the *Four Zoas* as well as his *Laocoön's* assertion that "Practice is Art   If you leave off you are lost." This motto of her youth continues to work in her old age. Her witchiness is not a choice but how she is seen by others. It is a strong, if vexed, position from which to work and see. Being old makes her aware of the nearness of death. She realizes she has begun a project and a practice that will take years to complete. She continues to begin.

WHICH WALK 0

re:assemblance

"Take a walk"
—YOKO ONO, *WALK PIECE*

and look out
as the broken world

breaks again
drawn to bits (I am)

               deranged   iota   jot

                    flakes   of fixed

                        whatnot

mechanisms meant
to broach when and where

to find or feel
a finite set with infinite

limitations as when
feast, fetish, or metonymic

gesture connects a personal
system with reference

to civic locality as
streets' vocal

versions of themselves,
when what is heard

is seen, gleaned,
recollected, and erected,

luck, self-
defined, becomes us,

bent into position feeling to find

       beads   balls   brass   steel

           nailed   screwed

       scaled up   run out

resurrected, inwardly

       directed to
       arrange and play
       as we (rapt)
       are carried off,

untroubled by resemblance,
guiding principle, or epistemic

framework, though having those,
while making these directed

acts of storage strutted,
glutted, taken up, as I/we

— 4

reaching back
to owned devices,

feel free, imaginary,
and tactile as the shudder

of daily acquisition,
domestic, time-bound,

vexed by practitioners,
whose practice

like ours,
a consummation,

is thrown up and out
as the poison

presence of each entrance
of nonlife into life

        twists   loops   moves

           circles   spits   and splits

        giving   into

          walking while

compromised by things
aging in place

as matter hardened to its
constituents is what

             we find when we amass and
             detach the past of an object
             from its fate creating
             an elegy for each fact,

used or not, whose provenance,
always one of loss,

rejection, and subsequent
stooping to find (oneself) with

items grounded by chance, labor
or the erasure of same

becomes stuff subject
to words like reality

adding up
to what we want:

an engine of past time,
creation, and abstraction

whose apparatus
reflects the precision of

                        wrapped   glass

           collapsed   threading   through

                    the fastness

of everything as everything
found or findable

resolves into action

WHICH WALK 1
for the Alices

"since there is time, some tea"
—DAWN LUNDY MARTIN, *Discipline*

broke the cup daily but
found (our love of)

tea was the project
with mourning and finding

what is lost or discarded to be
identical to specimens

whose depths steeped and
interrupted by concoctions

added to what is said to be
the eyebrows of a deity

        who we believe to be
        as musical as chairs when
        the sitters switch
        curious as children

whose terrible adventures
we think we know but

maybe don't as when
pressed against sense

or senses   five   or six

              pips   of a   divisive

card   despite   whose

              warnings

of mental   metal   stained

                  gist   kissed   with

heads headed inward and onward
following pedestrians present

only in the minds we know
to be among the lovers

of tea pictured here playing the game where downing the cup as a move
and a stance is seen to be the strange remnant of the imaginary past
present among the participants who agree only on tea

and being in this party
of one and others whose

smiles connive hovering over
gullets down which tea slides

enlivening the insides of the
insiders who finally go

farther than we knew we'd go
when we knew we'd go on

WHICH WALK 2
which who

and I have a public meaning
not always or even often

seen. There's no help to shirk
or quit until there is

and then being
becomes not only

who but where
you are, for a time.

I hear myself say

in a hard rhyme with my situation which has to do

with what is happening now

in what could be called the present past,
an event in the grammatological sense,

            meaning as a demonstration of
            parallel lives, as for example, that
            which is like whatever is intended

to wake, walk (or not) on this late morning

with its cold wind, its clarity
an essential factor without which

there is nothing but what is changeable
in the short definition of itself which,

again, like me, remains hidden
despite its endless iteration as a practice

accurate as can be conceived
by us who don't define our

condition in single terms,
not to mention shape, scape,

or other characteristics listed,
so controlled, however briefly,

with grim wit applied to the natural
and unnatural worlds where, drawing

on our familiar ache, we find ourselves
in the crucible of risk and wish,

the molten mirror of which, reveals
the muscular gait we assert while

    saying   as   playing

        marches   us   around

    until   that   cadence

by changing   creates

what is vast and uncontained like

a dance called out or as the call
and response of an air which

becomes the wind in the look see
place whose rhythm one affirms

as a being with claims to a territory
invisible as it is physical like the

flying that famously occurs or the
fricatives chanted by practitioners,

lit by the sun of night, as is said, or by
the daytime moon, present as vanishing.

          Let's be in this together,
          I think, of the gentle friends,
          hard as the nails I collect
          or the glass I crack,

the better to connect and see
words as actions, reading as facts

becoming that which is us

and me, framed by the sea, up against
the sky, love's mind, weirdly real

WHICH WALK 3
first love first

Anciently arrived by dint of sails
attached to skulls and brains

> (like us but unlike)
> (ours) smiling
> in the sun and wind by
> the crocodilian river with

warm blooded females (us) (me)
unsurprised by age and rage

Our psychic or psycho-sexual approach neutralized until time-of-day
or time-of-life arguments proposed in sun and shade smile among the
fronds lighting up our enormous brains among the gracefully extended
heat ridges on our heads and in our hearts where

I read the signs thriving
on attention or lack thereof

anticipating the moment
we align ourselves *vis à vis*,

predators, with nesting calculations
alive in our minds, achieve desire,

consensus, even love

WHICH WALK 4
title role

"It's my whim to walk"
—Vera Caspary, *Laura*

the killer observes to the detective
whose careful talk is also mentioned

in this melodrama of identity
confounded by moves which fool

us along with characters who
each take the measure of belief

                     in the other
                     as they distort
                     the story of Laura

whose troubled love of assertion argues
a wrong long since contained as if

a name was mistaken (by I of me)
or by a protagonist whose pensitivity

means to be taken up by time,
new again—real, but not true

now or then. We met at the movie. I was late. There was love and
betrayal. A hidden death. Clifton Webb was not British. Dana Andrews
wanted to sing, Gene Tierney to smoke. She lowered her voice. She wrote
poetry, was

—14

replaced only to reappear
at a critical time for the crime,

        left alive but
        guilty of failing or

falling, down, as with flying,
or out, as if in love with doubt

      linked   mint   meant

          still   ridge

                  sill

      window   light

because memory isn't like
the remembered life as

the present fills with thunder
with its following light

I hear my name change
when sung or played and realize

        the usual bind has occurred
        with its inevitable break as
        things go wrong leaving me

assured of the song and of going on

with ecstasy and pain whose
pause and refrain continue while

I, uncontained, named, and known
as flown, contrive to fly

WHICH WALK 5
the maid real

"Old Woman, your eye searches the field like a scythe!"
—ROBERT DUNCAN, "The Structure of Rime VI"

like a sigh, permitted or not,
these visits to Mira Vista

       Field   fair   farm   (or look see

            place)   which   with

      walking   later

         renounces   renunciation

         the better to incantate as
         phrase after praise betrays
         the visible day to the visible

night today singing what can you say,
moment by movement, or see

worried, wise, amazed—
heard, herded, heralded, crazed

by this old epithet, rule, and designation

         of hags for which read old
         women whose presence
         absent to some,

purely physical to others, despite being where
and what they/I, are required to be, go, say,

    and know   noting   how

        dreamed of   mental   meeting

    flit   born   stance

    best   is

    crash   crush

        daughter   whose

protocols in the form of songs and knowledge
combine the known with the read, said,
intoned, and suggested,

    along with the berries there, also
    red, thorns with which to be bled,
    leave one stepping out attired in

gown, crown, and scythe
clearing what has died into

what is born by the poem of the mind
including words not me but mine

while I, menaced by remembered threats,
summon my ways and those of my actual

mother, Mae Belle Reynolds,
to push in and back out while
hatted, masked, cloaked, fraught

being with her (withered) wrought

where   belief   relief

          knowing   & going   are brought

along with these steps at the feet of which laid

out, we, reconfigured into us,
write what is read, said, and

displayed, resolving the "made place"
into the made real day

WHICH WALK 6
problem of reversible time

"... which am I?"
—RUMI, *The Essential Rumi*

who (exigene)
portends to redeem

exigencies of a woman
and man in a van when

our names meant light, knight, air, and ones who fly (are flown) when
you, Sufi, carpenter, botanist, and me, writer, waitress, artist of cards
and fortunes, later lose our clothes on the way to losing our minds and
hearts (mine) in a known place where written as played

> a woman much withered, a maid,
> a maiden with a wand, a handsome
> maid, a white wand with a peacock of
> solid gold on its tip

(we) submit
to the reversible fortunes

of muscle memory and the
illusive person in the poem

including types of knowing as when

The Land That Time Forgot
or trip into symbolic space

—20

whose   trace   discloses

      beauty   at intervals   as   (not)

lucid   eyes

of mind remain blind to the
inevitable arrangement's

transformation of attitude,
and altitude calculable only from

the surface or search image
of a specific person

whose comparative anatomy
comes into play when the algorithm

leads us farther into the past—
but if this is the solution

       please explain the bones
       in the ghost story of the other
       lover or the card games there.

Bring in Propp's *Morphology of the Folktale*

and other extinction events.
It was crazy for anyone to try

to cross the Sierras in October.
What happens next as we

decohere among the hominins (despite
the abstraction, attraction, and object lessons)

is anybody's guess.

WHICH WALK 7
what and who

A dark day finds
heart's head hatted

and masked with crime
being read into its head

as descent into the local hell

means taking in the ashy
remains of everything with

each breath a reckoning, each step
the mistake of not sheltering in place

        while   elsewhere   breath

            taken   fills

the same head with fresh despair
of the deadly situation where seconds

            become minutes then
            centuries where the dead lay
            with vast fires closing in

but not here or not yet as
trying for a semblance

                   of thought   as active   leveraged

                          expression   of fair

                   weather's   familiar

talk while reassembling the same
everything in head's heart

of later air clear for now

though nothing is better
except if it is when

kinds of crime rhyme
what is wrong (but present)

with what (and who) are gone

WHICH WALK 8
the old return

from representation to an imagined
past requires tools knapped

according to cracks where
sensation alone might be enough

> to start as the craft spread,
> flake by flake, the everyday
> making of prosidized units
> while things and time brought us

to the place to which we aspired
when we got beyond ourselves

to facts like fire weather and wild
contact, with our exact love of walking

> continually   arriving   step by

>   fact   of backing   out onto

home ground where gesture precedes
articulation, meant to reflect from

the inside out fresh schemes
to generate kinetic expression

as when, abandoning short-term memories,
we set out into the yellow leaves on a

particular day, happy despite the vicissitudes,
able to predict, plan, execute, and review (but

not picture) the future where hunting and
gathering continue to be their own

                          ends until the spirals
                          visible on all our surfaces
                          reassert themselves

as the guaranteed repetition made
of death and space where we stand

mindfully outside the universe of words
reading them back to ourselves suspended

                          in the phantom of equilibrium
                          as if it was a drug or sigil

with bold hearts as a side-effect or
side-lined effect, as we later hold,

despite and because of our descent into

ecstatic time seconds before or beyond
an elsewhere from which we are never

disallowed because (and we knew it then)
we are the old ones now

Are there two lines because there are two feet, hands, eyes? Maybe. This walking and making is a process, a procession. When she called an earlier book *Symmetry* she meant to dismantle this concept with each gesture. Is this that? she wonders, but suspects it is not—as, falling endlessly forward, she moves through space like a sound or a bird. A need for trust occurs. Balance. Emptiness. You can't think about every step, but you should, she worries. Situational awareness. A military term. A thing is exact. Or exactly not. Intentional. Intended. Once her project was something like courtly love but now she feels betrothed to her work.

The woman stares at herself in the mirror. She makes self-portraits less because of an interest in self than because she is her only model. She enjoys drawing her wrinkles because they add texture. Me and not me, she is simply a thoughtful arrangement of phrases, lines, and planes— scribbled hair.

script   sent

scene   infers

              repeat   but

knot

WHICH WALK 9
look see time

"No one speaks Martian ..."
—JACK SPICER, *My Vocabulary Did This to Me*

but us whose rusted skies
drift over volcanoes higher

than Earthly ones but for the
just born, sporting, as they do,

plant life, false starts, and parallax

          views formed when a chance
          phrase changes like a snake
          into a bird dreamt by the world

whose confluence of bodies of water,
as rivers with rivers, "I with thee,"

birds with fruit with trees who
sing and say remembered

phrases called courtly meaning
flutes, bells, books of kells,

       calls   cauldrons   coverings

                as chrysalides   enfolding

      living   monarchs

whose commands are pronounced
by today's traipse into the sun and

shade of look see place
including what is created

by the panoply of responses
whose instrumentation

         allows us to think through
         the catastrophes as of famine
         and dread assimilated into
         a song inside a head sustained

by whistle and drum where bones
serve as flutes and bells as themselves

and all as the drone which hums

when we call each other Martians
we know what we mean and for

that moment what we want
when we read the book as if

we'd both written the prophecy
that exists in this transcription

of buds and bugs blossoming
as the field goes green

and those who know dream
hot of the Martian cold

       old   stint   brash

       cast   dint   of

                     exact

WHICH WALK 10
sound effect

or auditory hallucination
is nothing to worry about

> though picturing the refinery
> blown or guns going off as happens
> more often than one would

allow if allowing were
as loud as the voices in

> the chorus in which this
> one finds herself knowing
> that noise is normal or is

imagination writ loud
at best or at worst

an episode considered
only for what it suggests

> about self, song, and time
> just as migraine aura is
> said to be a second mind
> spiraling as it crosses

the blood brain barrier both
constructive and obliterative

of inner vision also called
mission drift made to seem

       too red   as blood   floods

         the site   a muted

       alarm   sounds

in the drugged inner brain

which when seen in person
during a procedure replacing

one lens for the other—
close with distant sight

seems safe, sound, and round
as when no beginning

means no end but passage
through if you can (while not dead)

read the stones whose
Ancient Use in Ray DiPalma's

       eponymous notebooks are
       delineated, mapped, framed
       and found even when "serenity"
       comes up "corrupted by its own music"

redolent of the script of
the movie whose victims

consumed by desire
remember themselves

as ancient lovers
by sound alone

an arrangement of notes
exchanged by poets

            until   one   disdains

                    the other's   hazy   online

            persona   as word's   version   vision

taken in vain when
all that's left of that
translation are those

perfectly arrayed forms
of knowledge and pain

WHICH WALK 11
first rain

"The sin is in the not doing"
—PAUL BLACKBURN, *The Journals*

"Selvage, that word" (same by same)
but what does it mean, anyway?

House finch sits with some
towhee whose tail spread and gray

        attests that this female can't
        not finish that book haunted
        by old calendars or folks

        whose assertions

kept us from madness committed
to that day's *Intimate Journal*'s

love of traveling new directions
with Roger Shattuck's *Banquet Years*

imitated by me hosting dinner parties in the tiny kitchen of the Haste
Street place where I had a cheap room with actors and poets. Jugglers.
It was a thing. Not unlike Xavier Martinez's spaghetti nights, as I later
learned. Modernism with its landscapes of thought. Tonalism with its
pink

air buds blossom with Crispell's *Amaryllis*

A woman avalanches down the street
(Karen Brodine) avalanching to the end

didn't make it out of the season when
betrayed by one's body as sure

as rain or no rain where
a shivering but warm wind

persists into a shared reading
of us Modernists lost

          in overcoats worn with summer
          cottons as we walked and danced
          composing out the window poems

whose juggled text meant
everything then like

the crow on the birch or that big jay

blends with heaven
thinks with wings

WHICH WALK 11 (alternate)
a light

"A bone has obligations"
—EMILY DICKINSON, *Collected Poems*

whose bolt of cloth, lightning,
melody, or memory's knights spoke

                    a dead language revamped
                    to be heard while occasional
                    sprites alight decamping
                    to gather where we

"dream in character" of mad love
of reading writing brightly

believing in nothing so much as
this vocation's fervent situation

all day gone
no way back down

                    again   against

                              sits

                                            dust

                    display   site

                    cited   sees

                    beyond

WHICH WALK 12
of use and power

realms we enter or pour over
with paint, cloth, paper,

       blank   printed   woven

          sewn   thrown

       like pots   wound like wire

devices as items of use and power
are found to go round like

       screws   twist   or washers

        gleam   often   in their

      shining

circles caught by crows swooping
down not unlike oneself drawn to

this moment's *memento mori*

because remembering to die is
not the same as to live for now

as what is preserved by these pots
including seeds that have passed

some sacred gut—action objects
broken now whose edges worn

by the sea cut, not the hand, but
the thoughts of what they were

before being tossed, like us, out
until we renegotiate the deal

                                         alert to any genii or beanstalk
                                         talk as when edging beyond
                                         sense we split the attention
                                         of magician, client, and victim

who or which might, by this craft,
be seen as written or known to be

what we expect to read, wear,
play, see, and believe of the future,

otherwise known as the solution,
though not for us, or only just

                  red   as   anything

                       spreads   when

                events   cause

                     themselves

WHICH WALK 13
of birds and earth

"the elegant flower
of which"
—LORINE NIEDECKER, *Collected Works*

appears in the thickets
whose steady readiness

measures the commotion
it is impossible not to feel

as when "bacteria don't know
they're bacteria" but do know

they're real as mental constructs
allow us (me) to execute

                this reasoned   optimistic   screech

                    of idea   discovered

to be taken up and written down

in a new older hand braced
with feral neurons checking

that I am all there, finding

I am measured in milliseconds
while humming the bird brain

song of the present
whose tiny bones
nested in big biomes
wind down to earth where

bereft we collect their sky-like
        cracked, speckled, faded,
        abandoned, and fragile shells

finding what's lost
with what's left

        best   by   some

                already   expired

        timing   beyond   whose

                try   again   gesture

        produces   what   wanders   past

                last

She falls. She has always fallen, just as people she has known have sometimes died. But not as often as now. One can fall at any time, tricked by gravel or uneven ground. People are at risk when they walk. Some more than others. They can be felled by other people or by cops. It's just luck to get old or fate, to be healthy enough to walk. An accident. An aporia. This is not pretended doubt but the real thing. She has always been in love with doubt.

There is a constant unmaking of self in writing or in making art. She wonders about old choices. Should she choose them again? The circumstances beyond her control are the usual ones. There are dangers but being old gives her the time to think and make. Dues paid. Walk away.

"We all get to a fuck it point of life. A moment worthy of celebration." Dolores Dorantes, translated by Facebook.

WHICH WALK 14
re:collection

"from the heart, from the body, from nature"
—SUSAN STEWART, *On Longing*

I go, masked,

to the recycling center, open after being closed for Covid and smoke
from endless fires. I don't see what I want, but, in a bin, observe a book
I read as a child on summer afternoons in the house of family friends in
North Falmouth—part of a series called *Childcraft*. Diving in, I reach
the book but it's the wrong one so, throwing it back, I step away, feeling
a sharp pain in my side. Later, I locate the book online and, finally, get
Childcraft, Volume Eight, Creative Play and Hobbies, Field Enterprises,
Chicago, 1949

What should I do now?
You can find a hobby.

You can't go wrong
whatever you study

you find a name, and
a place, a history

of things injured by
more time than we

deserved for the
victimless crime of this

remembered forgetting
of broken objects,
uncreated, but found in the
world as quarry whose

queries abound as for example:
what accelerant beyond the air

will hasten the decay of this
"garbage strewn plenitude" (Susan Sontag)

    grit   girded   gimcrack

        appendage   upended by

    baseline   or boxed   present

whose tracks in the brain
like the ones from pain in mine

bright white areas

of headaches caused by
existing in any way

at any time, migraines for which
I am about to give myself

a shot of salvation

        as when daily expeditions
        produce loot, booty, information,
        color, texture, shape, design,
        duration, cyclicality, the recent future,

and the plain past all visible in the
constant revision, realization,

"haptic reconnaissance" (William Gibson)

and combination of the material in
question. Steel, zinc, chrome, tin,

iron, plastic, and glass, and such else
as is wanted in the moment,

placed as they are, not yet glued
or fastened, but always often

revised and revealed by
keeping track with a pointless

but determined fascination,
not unlike the stratigrapher

                who falsely found the border
                of El Cerrito and Richmond
                at Cutting beneath the big rock once
                visible from the bay long since

blown to bits, some of which might
be part of the fireplace in this house

or its foundation at whose pure point
a woman across the world says
to her son of her threatened home
"There is nowhere to go. Die here with me."

The fire this time is the fight also now
of plagued, changed, fearfully arranged

claims, minerals, concrete, polymers,
and other substances sublated into each

    grave   bone   bag   born

        shown   longed for

  state   of being

      known   then gone

a common temporality, a mechanical genesis
and fossil whose social status

      as the nonalive artifact
      celebrated here where

I go masked and have gone

with the real thing as image
its holy hope intact

as a nonfiction system

found in the debris of leavings
making me into you or you me

depending on how one sees, dreams,
or feels what almost doesn't exist

yet persists

WHICH WALK 15

no future

" . . . no future but itself"
—EMILY DICKINSON, *Collected Poems*

in another state

or time zone
with its lullaby of fortitude and

        geontological persuasion,
        gerontolgical power notwithstanding,

"biopolitics [is] increasingly subtended by geology"

Yusoff, *Geological Subjects*
Elizabeth A. Povinelli

The apposite and aforementioned
geontology being a bold retheorization

of life and non-life, including the vexed

and perhaps hexed entanglement
of old ways of thinking with those that,

also old, have gotten us into
the present extinctions

as we gerontologically challenged
survivors might remind

        our already fucked selves
        that we possess no time
        to get right what is beyond

this atlas of human tectonics
falling into place around

what are known to be rare
earth elements whose magnets

        catalyze   what

                exceeds   that which

        passes   for action

is acceptable in this domestic context
despite the warning of glass and bone

breakage including their legibility,
effect, and affect as

        those of us with home labs can
        attest to when we experiment
        hidden from the burning of what passes
        for air around here bending again

into machines as if the divine
accordionist was to squeeze

the sublime air directly
into the brains of us makers whose

"space is the arena of direction, velocity, variables"
Carolyn White, *The Archaeology of Burning Man*

and whose practice is located
where time as bottleneck

is recognized as the
predicament from which

we are going nowhere as fast
as we can and where further

she (we) I collect information,
friends, events, images, and moves

while researching
whatever comes next

on this planet where one quarter
of everyone has a collection of

something of which they want
a complete set as for example of

bricks, lists, lace, fans, guns,
puns, books, or places

"The oddest poetry book collector I've known was a guy who worked
at GCHQ in Cheltenham. I mean oddest in his method. Let's say he

bought a book by X published by a press called P. He'd then want every book by X as well as all the publications of P. Assuming that X was also published by other presses, he'd now want all their publications too, as well as all other books by every poet they published. And so on, exponentially. Nobody could actually read that amount of books but I was never sure he read any. Although it certainly meant he bought large quantities on his at least monthly visits. . ." Alan Halsey, correspondence

which competitive practice
of amassment extends to

the body of the collector or celebrant
as oneself with one's cards, figurines,

charms, and puppets. No one knows who
invented the puppet. Or the charm.

    Is this about harm, reinvention,
    radios, robots, razors, glass—
    things that might bite back? Sharps.
    Object logic with a will emerging

as a collection of its former selves.
The pile, heap, mound, midden of

metal boxes whose index cards
tell the history of museums and

disciplines, present in our
minds with their notions

of complicity, intransigence, and
the will to survive as by sheer desire

she dreams the boxes and wakes up arranging them in her mind, indi-
vidually and in groups. There is a tiny figure. She assumes it's a version
of herself but thinks of it as him, the little guy. He is made of aluminum
wire, as if drawn with one line. She wears him as a charm on a chain.
His figure appears in the inmost section of a plexiglass box of many
chambers, not unlike the pill box by the bed of the now rarely taken
migraine med, or the nautilus

which leaves the "low-vaulted past"
to join the world filled, as in

choked, with images that
Oliver Wendell Holmes Sr.

> could not have imagined or
> swallowed. Not "webs of living
> gauze," but nonalive circuits, bits
> of whatever dead thing can be

enlivened with this process,
whose restlessness needs limits

to keep from rolling away,
and becoming illegible even

to the ones who, like me,
love them so. It so.

WHICH WALK 16

but what is steel

if not the most
recyclable of materials?

Iron ore into pig iron
worked in the forge or lab

or on the table complete with
paper made into a fan

or a face spread out like
a map or sledgehammer

        pictured here with the other tools
        we find and use more to break
        than to build though that too.

Fine, flat, or round-nose, pliers, wire
cutters, scissors, awls, threaders

    mothers of   glass   classic

      shell's   pearl   whirls

  born   of   excretion   and belief in

    keeping to

sledge meaning to strike with slag,
slay, and slog connected,

not as meaning but
as associative assembly

of detritus like
Damascus steel or silk

whose pattern of
overlapping ornament

of simple stars, golden angles,
and Fibonacci series of

                          spiralized receptacles
                          contain lost chords,
                          water, ether, and the cosmos

allowing us to declare with
Michelangelo Frammartino that

"We are minerals"
fixed in a microbial

                          matrix of fear, aversion,
                          shells, hells, bits of the future or

lack of one in which we
read and see our steely fate

"Assemblages are ad hoc groupings of diverse elements, of vibrant materials of all sorts. Assemblages are living, throbbing confederations that are able to function despite the persistent presence of energies that confound them from within."

Jane Bennett quotes Deleuze and
Guattari in *Vibrant Matter* as

self-ordering forces emerge
from within without warning

or intuition to reveal the finite
aspect of each thing being

slightly off, its electricity a cluster
of charged parts producing

a smooth synthesis of sound
as an aurality blown, beaten, or plucked

predicts the metal
present like a curse

which flows into the debris
of metallic sonority

as when cymbals clash and
hiss audibly from where

the metallurgist steps back
into the intelligible essence

of the Venusian kiss
fondly offered here

— 54

WHICH WALK 17

And what is Venus
if not the good which

> enters the mechanosphere
> breathfully permeating
> the social field,
> enveloping a stratum

of product and process
that like a virus gets

in your head, drawers, bureaus,
boxes, and other receptacles

> resulting in tool use,
> digging up, and putting out
> an array of Galileo's Balls,
> loose stainless-steel spheres

in clear boxes segmented by size,
beauty, delight, and contrivance

"This morning I stretched out/in an urn of water /and like a relic /rested"
                    Giuseppe Ungaretti, tr by Geoffrey Brock

but not rusted as this
melting pot of metal

slopping as we walk, alters
the cognitive tools used by

a community of practitioners
whose desire to know

demands that we ask
what is our consensus?

Do we exist in the overlap
of our repertoires?

"common concepts, acknowledged
statements, recognized problems"?

Manuel DeLanda
Assemblage Theory

          The taxonomy of the deal
          surrenders to the phenomenon
          of new experiments whose results
          remain unknown beyond being

"Nothing That Is Not There
and the Nothing That Is"

Wallace Stevens by way of Peter V. Swendsen
Allusions to Seasons and Weather

facing field out, recorder in hand,
devised, organized—

includes the archives—
as part of the equipment of

         lab   bag   party   gang

              scene   set

         assembly   studio   garage

            band   cluster of

garbage or waste, as of things or time. Our words are our destinations.
Debris debrided from gutters, pockets, placed in Ziplocs as she/I walk
toward while walking away, over identical streets and trails, bending to
examine items dropped, lost, or left. Standing erect, hands free, brain
changed by this activity

to a circle of crows
which scold as I stoop

into bits crowded
like bugs or other beings

            possessing the power to
            sting, bite, transfix,
            swarm, charm, alarm,
            curse, or fend off

the bad luck in which
we don't believe as we

gather up or leave behind
whatever it is we, in the

form of me, think
we are doing with this

        cursed   hacked   tactical

            hagiography   tagged

       with fever   fury   revealed

          receipted   received

into an ancient person who
might organize their world

by suspending something
from a body part or

just by putting it out there
as an abstract machine

"of singularities and traits
deduced from the flow"

Deleuze and Guattari,
not born yet, in retrospect,

devise the definition
as products of a process

                    supple, rigid, legible,
                    accelerated, ruptured, shown

to be an undefended
territoriality spreading out

over an unincorporated part of
Contra Costa County from

a mind troubled with the
collective unconscious of age

and the fungible cosmology
of youth when like a specter

                    with silver hair we wander,
                    collect, assemble, and remember
                    what might explain who did
                    this why then or is doing it now.

Veins of gold and iron threaded
through the universe from its hot

density at the beginning to the
current metamorphic state where

what builds up, burgeons on,
breaking down into

something like the stellar object
observed by us as if it was

the aspiration of how far one can
go with something one can make

or do, of which experience
itself is a grid of random

sanity imposing a temporary
order to an old problem

        knot   deeply   amazed

            and discussed   spiral

        design   grid   incised

in stones ruined
well before

this book of activities first
opened itself to you

WHICH WALK 18

"Things base and vile"
—WILLIAM SHAKESPEARE, *A Midsummer Night's Dream*

on the sidewalk being
attached to the ground

       as oneself

           floats   falling

     over   moving   forth

           by gravity   appreciating

every inch of the concrete
verge whose presumed

safety is abandoned when we
take to the street in order to

breathe but not on others
despite being in the most

vaccinated, also called, the Golden
State, not burning yet, sheltered

           by June gloom we proceed with
           local creatures through the clear

dry world giving each other
space while scavenging washers

and nuts in my case and in theirs
nuts and berries. Both (all)

recognize refuse as potentially
relevant though requiring quick

thought as we/they radiate out
beyond accustomed ranges

examining the new with a view
to what might advance while

enhancing the way thereby locating

    a dragon   charm   whose lobster

        clip's   frayed copper   element's

    perfectly   faceted   flake

comprises yesterday's take
which finds a place in being

the goal of this attachment
as me of it in mine

WHICH WALK 19

rapt glass

assumes the walker
urban, nocturnal who

by night or dreamy day drifts
past work-related concerns

              to glance thingward
              noting the random gleam
              of a made place
              whose temporary situation

rhymes with the known
precarity of life lived

with unknown lives
clustered in and outside

of risk which doesn't stop
anyone from doing anything

              despite being fixed, broken,
              fixed again, and in suspense

thick with connected bliss
including of being

            shut in   cut   adorned

fused   splayed and   arrayed

        whose   insistent

unresolved story unscrolled and

wired into consummation
distracted by containment

is directly aimed at doing
without within the context

of traveling through
diagrams imposed by

        found   rusted   opaque

           maps of   skeletonized

sunlight radiating into rapt
windows and glassy eyes

        passing by the same
        place at the same time
        obligated by the moment's
        existence to keep

oblique while maintaining
a familiar distance

coincident with being
carried away

—64

by the timeline made
anomalous by the everyday

aspect of the ongoing problem
of what could possibly be meant

by what is happening now

WHICH WALK 20

I walk

"I walk the unbelieving streets"
—JACK SPICER, *My Vocabulary Did This to Me*

guided by mind

from inner to outer
space and time, oneself

as reassigned, resigned
to customs of place

> and brain whose veins
> clear of the familial
> threat of abrupt failure
> per grueling tests

which, having passed, left
one's corpus rife with

nervy vigilance despite
free capillaries' momentous

flow, making the walk
while walking, the list,

while listening
to the history of tints

                rare   as ruby   glass

                        hued   blues   common

                as mood   threaded   through

colors of air and sky
to apprehend the bright

locomotion located
in a head from which

a body depends
like a line extended

                        further and faster out
                        for the sheer fuck of thought
                        generated action maximizing

today's walk's effect
of keeping things level

                        headed   while   each

                                step's   inner

                        mechanisms   rhyme

with each deft
retention of time kept

while continuing to fall
out if not down resolutely

      managing   vicissitudes   of cats

      dog moans   clack   of birds

        barriers   apples   books

      vases   free   abandoned

as frames fastened into

a perspective display
of rapture, attachment, and

glassy clarity gridded into
hive-like wire opening

onto the aforementioned brain's perfect
parade on and down the streets away

      stained   yet   vetted

        vast   as   the strange

      mechanic   who   stayed to

        execute   the play

The woman walks in and out of the fallen world, collecting broken shells from the birds with whom she shares the air. She is followed by ghosts. Crows are of particular interest. Seeing themselves in her large black hat, they scold. She thinks of them as Apollo's birds, resisting their morbid reputation. Which of us doesn't survive on carrion?

"Old age is a radical situation," she reads in Anne Truitt's journal. "Time will eventually arrive at my door." When she wrote those lines, Truitt was a decade older than the woman is now. She keeps track. This one is younger, that one older, or the other one already dead.

Occasionally cars, or more often trucks, go by, driven by guys who, oblivious to age, check her out or even stop leeringly to ask the way. She is amused to realize she is probably older than their mothers, no, grandmothers! Which puts her in mind of an ill-advised walk she once took down Polk Street in pursuit of some random crush of the 70s. As she entered the Tenderloin part of that stroll, somewhere around Turk, she remembers the cars pausing, the men in them, based on their ribald questions, assuming her to be a sex worker, despite the glasses. She knows she was lucky to get out of that situation alive and uninjured. What was she thinking? What is she thinking now?

That this is one of her stories. Like the one about hitchhiking and the sailors. Bad decisions. Being a hayseed in her hayseed finery. Reading Sappho. Being in love with her mentor. Teacher. Lover. Predator. Being twenty harder than being seventy. What is true? she compulsively wonders, as she draws the street, her face and hat, the trees. Goes back out. Dreams aloud of ghosts   which   ask

           with   familiar   gasp

why   we are   (not)

WHICH WALK 21

of ancient

"wild witches . . ."
—WILLIAM BUTLER YEATS, *Collected Poems*

whose ritual with skill,
information, and liminal

linking of water, trees, and weedy

wisdom faced with
head emphasis as

           the head for the person
           or for deaths' descending
           attention to place, speech,
           seasons, songs, lakes

or loughs from which
appear massive carnyces

trumpet-like with lotus pattern
from Egypt via Eastern Europe

more a style than a plan,
an attitude than an

articulated mode though
found with battle gilded

crown   cauldron   cup

      axe   charm

    coin   held   form

should tell of horned
persons fought, patterns

deployed of knots, bowls, pots,
swords, and torcs with ravens, owls,

and bulls hoarded then
thrown into bodies of water

        known barely to contain
        deities whose deeds
        pictured as gifts and tricks
        are ones whose agendas

interact in medley form,
sung to be strung out along

roads and coasts becoming
fast sad pieces with which

        to stand   see   and stomp

          in place   where   fate

       footed

ghosts featured in controlled
forays of wild competition

ridden, fiddled, riddled
with oaths sworn and air

squeezed from devices that
seem to breathe on their own

as rivers flow into rivers'

improvised spells are recast
as blessings quickened with

friends and endless
kin in the midst of lives

and deaths carved into
still standing megaliths

lit tonight while time
fits into the promised

recognition and threat
of preowned gestures

whose best repetition

handheld   unwritten

pretense   of honeyed

metal   fits exactly

into the predicted existence
as a flowering circle

made of stone fully
"by our devices known"

emerges as home

WHICH WALK 22

felt flowers

IN MEMORY OF PAM ROBINSON

Attachment to practice
promises action's

like-minded advance only
to return, dissatisfied,

      retiring gradually,
      not at all, or suddenly,
      before beginning again
      with each act connected

but closed off like a
necklace or a pendent

with powers, or a premise
without them, including

the fact of itself and nothing
else but whatever is

     torn   delineated   contracted

      deducted   doubted   attacked

and finally detached
by age and frailty

declining while the inevitable
detritus of living threatens

life with being cut, pierced,
or otherwise altered

as I/you are carried away

despite and because
of the will to attach

artificial objects of glass,
plastic, paper, wire,

        and desire or, better, felt—
        than which what else best
        suggests the warmth of flesh
        and flowers dying while admired

as natural by us as we mourn
in advance of yet another collapse

of living into life
not going on

      now   when   being

           meant   the past

      present   resolves into

          strings   in late

      afternoon   time when

         beauty   then

WHICH WALK 23

that collecting staves off
or in any way affects death

or the future is not provable
by me or mine which

is saved barely long enough
to be seen though the suggestion

that by this practice time becomes
material is exactly right

        as arranged and stuck by glue,
        wire, and in broken lines, their
        wanting and having reliably

provides a finders' glee lending
themselves to further fictions

as well as the need for

        organization   storage   style

          designated   useful   only

       for a while   before   being

discarded like the wrong card.
It is well to have started late

in this gathering and making whose

objects, as specimens and evidence,
are located on a conceptual grid

representing an actual place
in my head as well as in

my garage where they
are attached to knotted wire,

heaped in containers,
arranged in tiny boxes,

and on tables, themselves
encountered by sheer chance

in their recycled glory
putting me in mind of

a gig at Atthowe Fine Art Services when, decades ago, in between jobs, I
took on the task of entering art into their data base, fascinated by their
warehouse of stuff, and by the arranging and keeping track that, look-
ing back, was the central action of my professional life. I liked being
praised by them, though absurdly overqualified for the job, which I left
soon after, for an equally brief stay at Innovative Interfaces where I was
the one you'd reach if your entire library system was down, eager to be
told by me to turn it off, then turn it on.

Fun was not involved then
unlike now when it's common

for me to get glad by finding,
breaking, and filing down

broken glass careful
to document, reveal,

class, and sort the debris left by both
breakage and the fact of piling up

       bent   scrounged   fastened

          pasted   scattered

      and flattened

junk as my erstwhile studio assembles
itself around the making, seen

as a sort of lateral transformation
of stuff into "the semantic realm of the box"

which proposes that phone shots
and text enliven the inanimate

as we plot the atlas of their
scarred passing from waste

to what I admit to picturing
as radios informing us of how

things worsen by the day then

end, further reminding
us, along with Duchamp,
that, distracted by the facts,
we "will completely disappear"

whether by fires, viruses, climate
collapse, or fuck all, meaning age,

going in and out of spaces
closed but open to chaos

with its predictable distress
and accurate thought

that this ecstatic creation
will be enough, until it's not

WHICH WALK 24

fiercely transpiring

Late summer life deludes
and delights as one leaf

of the silver birch turns
to gold causing me to pose

the question of what it
means to despair of

or ignore the collapse predicted
in 2040 by a random scientist.

> "But what does he know?"
> demands Steve whose love
> of facts, affords us the pleasure
> of moving past the future

into the present moment
of attaching only to detach

> glass, breaking down what is
> assembled, enmeshed, and up-
> ended in the studio in my brain

found to be almost but not the same
as the one being made

as when the local coyotes eat pet cats to transfer domestic moisture into
their feral gullets. Coyote behavior is often mentioned on the Next
Door email list by pet owners who fear these predators as they trot along,
deadly but cheerful, like the glass I find

sharp, shining, broken, ultimately
fixed into a pattern that provokes

> a tendency toward the old
> divinations I falsely feel
> to be the luck we concede

is the crux of the narrative
also false or at least contrary

to the prepandemic tenets
to which I adhered back

when a lot happened and we got here—

> to early autumn's late morning rain,
> fulfilling dreams of heat reduction
> and drought busting precipitation
> which however has created

the problem of me sliding down
steep hills on slick streets in yet

another demonstration that aging
is hilarious. A bay away, Norma

is finally getting out on walks

— 82

with Susan and Steve, healing

from an August procedure in
what is now fully fall, our visions

meanwhile blurred by steady rain on
closed windows that reveal, in my case,

the birch to be laced with more
gold than ever or let's call it the

        lemon   blond   flaxen

            straw   light

       gilded   aureate

yellow of the oriole
I saw yesterday or

of today's goldfinch
bright like cut flowers

fiercely transpiring

water and light
alive for now

WHICH WALK 25

the wild corollaries

After Alice Coltrane's *Journey in Satchidananda*

of going but remaining
in the same place whose

glassy tears don't
have to mean

sadness but do
blurring sight swells

as listening with eyes
minus cataracts

with lenses added
as multiple vision's

              delusive repetition replaces
              single sight with at least
              double the desire:
              for a clear sky, a heart free

from lies, a psyche from
hate, as something

like grace surprises even me
as even I wake with a sense

                of scale   which   changes

                    healing   fully   when

            fleet   peace

determines which walk is next
resting into steps, departures,

                    and circlings back arriving with
                    belief intact as a matter of urgent
                    fact with its pluck and strumming
                    notes of angelic revery

a refuge whose protection
includes the strange success

of going on by going
out, despite everything,

beyond doubt into sound,
with its wild corollaries

WHICH WALK 26

more on fate

as today's for me involves
making things into

"ambivalent, paradoxical, ironic and serious"

arrangements with (or as)
collaboratively determined

ways to mean whose relics

      and   racks   are stacked

           fastened   found

     detached despite

being tumbled together with
buried objects the desire

for which obtains among
the metal discs, single earrings,

      or wires bent to unlock cars
      where cognition is a hiddenness
      persisting within the spark of ignition

demonstrating loss which,
like a game, laid out to play,

—86

wear, eat, and see, means
an old thing in a language

new to me for being legible
to you. All of which remains

to be gleaned and seen
as an homage to the day,

whose solace is an invocation
to what is inevitable but

unacknowledged as fate exists
in the prismatic conditions

of its shattered persistence,
along with this bliss

WHICH WALK 27

this bliss

being the last word
of the last poem

predicts the excessive
brightness against watery

sockets quivering in this fresh
phase of being twenty twenty

not the year or age
but the sight as always

        only as available as
        the moment which falls
        around shoulders exposed
        to the inclement heat's

unguarded moment of
sun whose rays and other

dangers, to young you and
old me, displace the warmth

we mean to feel in this time
of going without knowing

which cohort I'm in or that my first
work appeared in *Nevermind*

nevermore   alerted   alike in

          displaced   but

     frightful   findings   as when

I of the so-called me
generation was me or

was I then and am now
this next feeling felt

                    while walking up and down
                    the block on the trail of
                    the familiar plot of the night's
                    person who wakes to find

themselves absorbed into a brilliant
darkness reflecting "These things [as]

superficial accidents . . . experienced by walking but not by feeling."

Bernardo Soares wrote adding
"The universe is not mine. It is me."

WHICH WALK 28

this peace (complete with)

the need to express love
or regret for the world

or not the world but us
in it, vanishing into ordinary

death as expected, or pandemic or
other planetary fails, personal falls,

threats, aggression, crimes, or faults causing

       silver alerts   chimed   on phones

       beside   or beyond us

       being   admittedly   frail

but persevering anyway into what

is known to be penetrable by sun
and thought altered by nothing

but walking on, standing by,
and wandering into dawn

       celebrating the gift of making it
       this far while the friends co-exist

with their beauty, regard,
and knowledge, as love's heft

becomes screen, page, scroll,
and what is left buckles, sagging,

its glass replaced by examples
of itself, allowing me to see

the livid yellow light

of the inherited pot not unlike
the goldfinch belly or the notebook

called "notes at night" dictated by
televised assertions of known
artists as Thomas Hirschhorn's
"Energy: Yes! Quality: No!"

admonition which persists
next morning intact

when waking into the physicality
of blood on the glass and

twisted actions make this
piece weighty and fragile

as what can't be diminished
by being read or said despite its

being legible, audible, hard
won, and always almost done

the case

The present is blurred or perhaps smeared across the page. Filled with desire. She lives by the seasons whose perspective is never quite right. The pictures behind her eyes emerge. The one of her face, the other of a place she was in, the objects there, the light. Each one many times. She longs for the cafes of her youth but prefers the tablets, tables, and trails of the moment. The work. Its blots and curves. Unexpected evidence of everything. "I get stronger as I get older," she wrote as a young woman. "But never strong enough."

The case stays open. She reviews her options, asking herself again what is true as she often used to do. Despite delusions and obsessions, she knew it then. Knows it now. She recognizes this as her main skill. Figuring it out, she moves on through

but finds that what is true needs to be refigured. What now? Will the book by the long dead artist she has ordered, out for delivery, explain everything? It materializes and sure enough she sees what to do in terms of color, music, and circles. In all their lovely ways. Chaos is involved. "Will the circle," she sings to herself, thinking of death, of various deaths, with fondness and trepidation. Colors of oil, water, pencils, objects, eyes, skin, life. As often, she listens to *Divine Love* by Leo Smith, before, she always enjoys thinking, he was Wadada. That "love" meaning there are sounds in this music that untune the universe. But no that's not right, she thinks, recalling the title of an old book. It's the sky.

whose   horizon   size   map

score   peak   page   gap

circles back   to find   defining   not to be

        entirely   without cost

WHICH WALK 29

upside down

which as (I is)

this pronoun which profiles
a thing in atemporal relation

> to another thing or one and
> as such reduces the deixis
> assumed by the self to be
> its due while reflecting

out like a shield or mirror and

in like an eye that sees in reverse
those other selves including those

with her (me) as again withered but
semantically active as our articulated

lives'   cumulative   threats

convey   a dangerous

but celebratory   demonstration

of things made of still more things
fastened with wire and string as part of

the being in question (me but not me)
contrives her way through the grid

of the poem and the missed of mourning
while people and opportunities self-create

with some dancing because they can
while others cling to situations and

people kept close because the political
is familiar and discourses thick

with what is hidden meaning
what the look see place hears

       individual sounds resounding
       into not quite songs as real as
       what goes on when you see me
       here or I you with our mind's heart

not forgetting doubts which further
surround what we know to be

the source of the sorcerer whose
spells melt in our hungry mouths

as the sun in the sea,
the moon anywhere

WHICH WALK 30

fleeing to fly

"...through the fog and filthy air"
—WILLIAM SHAKESPEARE, *Macbeth*

and when again   to repair   consort

being already   there   brought by flight

sky wise   gone to where   counted, spread,

courted, distorted by winged things whose stark

dark as Corvidae brightly go looking to declaim

Apollo's sweet, birded show of flow, flutter, float,

and crow, as maven, raven, and jay's jagged heap of

words known to be god-aligned, beaked, bound

nightly flown   through jeweled corridors

of night's day's   pleasured   way of gifting

love's surprise   held by   swift lifting's

flight as mind   hot to climb

sinking to rise, wake, fail, fall, and dive

—96

hawk-like into   sound as flight

flight as mind's   instance of being found

(out) aloft, alert, awake, and alive, riding, flying,

having flown,   not alone, not without

muscle's motion's deft gesture of going in by going out

inside life's   bright proposal

of outside bones   hollow, hallowed, haloed,

hosted, dark eyed,   sight, gone and going,

knowing exactly   what it's like to know

WHICH WALK 31

varieties of which

"Oh, that I could fly . . "
—WILLIAM JAMES

as charms of finches, diaries
of doves, and other avians
hover, humming down into,
hunger, delight, and desire
having gone as oneself
around, finding who or what
holds the breast pressed by
feral prayer into folds of
the heart's feathered weather's
beating declaration of being
free and aware of the heft
of iridescence in the very air
followed by day's wary insight
into staying high while abiding
being equivalent to not dying
which is, in turn and time,
the same as flying

WHICH WALK 32

which contortionist's

quick twisting though

becalmed   becomes   the jump

allowing herself   with all the senses

to be sprung from memory named as

heart not head declaims the muscular

            "Here we go"

launch announcement

taking off as arriving without content

or motion notion   that flight is like

what falls the air around

and apart   not stopping

nothing   but the crew whose

true story   of drift is

consonant with lift not being actual except as

what happens when   the mind dives

dividing itself into what are you now if not

the robin of dark days or light nights which

as viewing, hover while humming to watch

what on a cliff above   a casually steep

street takes, with green throated thought, off as we

spread ourselves, without delay, out, to drop through

bird lovers, tree huggers, house proud neighbors

staying down while staying up

beyond the cars   nearby sparkling

on the freeway   through massive

oaks thriving   on the divide between

what's real but   hidden as the mage in

imagination applies to the acrobatic connotations

stuck until now to a place like an emotion

applied to the pages   piled on the table

and in the lines of the flyer

as defining what of we we cause ourselves to be

when this witch commits to action comprising

breath, death, seething,   and seeing, seeks

all other senses   sending to find

the guaranteed good time known to be

winding past gravity's ruination of flight's

collapse into plain day   or mere night despite

the boundlessness whose creatures can be

spied amidst the fiery north wind's

warning of being   blindly true to

a harsh argument's

will to stay in the face of which, flying

anyway, knowing this going to be wanted

for self and others whose leaps of grace taken

as the not being kept down for long slogan

resolves to notes written, played, and shown

as this day's illumination

keeps track of this   tetragramatonic

time whose   flight reads real

when flying is flowing   knowing that going

is gone and (to have)   flown is home

WHICH WALK 33

gone because

when fly meant to flee

from famine, arrest, war, or general cursedness of

the local imperium's machinations we did and do

ending up gone   to a new but old hemisphere

not here but   back east or Midwest

in time to fight   the Civil War on the Minnesota

side or to arrive   in Providence as a freshly

hitched orphan bride   whose new names rhyme

with the new time   and whose chair rocked

as she drank while not failing to fall, rustling in her silk, doing

(or not) what she was compelled to do while flying (not even)

trying to answer the question of what to have done not to die so young

As what can anyone do faced with the nothing of today's masked

wandering against the world despite being exactly like what of it

there is or was as flying is dying to be born away

with the function words we know

the pronouns we own

WHICH WALK 34

which crew's

"elated symmetry of flight"
—MINA LOY, *The Lost Lunar Baedecker*

falls flying true to our

trajectory's tragic dive's

shifting life pictured   coherent with

not being   actual except

as one is   congruent with

the horizon of what happens when the mind arrives

finally to wind itself   into glass framed

sky filled with moonlight invisible to unawakened eyes,

as for example, mine   whose silver birch,

waning stars, and wavering falls hover while heralding

that which, on a street, teeters beyond yet another cliff

floating past the future accessible only to jewel-throated

gestures through which we persist dropping directly

down through trees hunting ourselves as hawks

also hover and dive straining to stay high while keeping

low deigning   to thrive on the timely

resistance of escaping   the misogynist mind

without which we   go beyond hiding by rising

into the godforsaken sky as fast flying, undisguised, goddess like she/I

unseen though stalked, mocked, thought it better to have walked

because grounded   though also did and further was

left to rise above   gravity and despair

(skylit in the naked air)   aware, aloft, and alive

because of love

She imagines the work she is doing is representational, but it isn't. It is gesture, even, ritual. There is a slantedness, in the Dickinsonian sense, a value for truth and idiosyncrasy—perhaps in the way of the slant step of her long ago heroes and teachers, the Bay Area artists who were her first living ones. They worked in a figurative way she sees as what is happening now in her own practice. The slantedness in her mind abides, the perspective. Life itself bent by hand—drawn, lined, sketched out—as it breaks into day. At night, creation opens up, causing her to fall or fly and, with a learned discipline, to rest and wait. Count her breaths and wait to wake.

So she drifts, drugged by the beauty of the quotidian whose rendering comprises a present that obliterates time. Or its's the future arriving with its demands. Or the present times out. The *Slant Step*, found in a Marin thrift shop by William T. Wiley in 1965, was designed for elimination, which, yes, is just another word for daily life's

incipient	shit	show	which
rhymes	when	the shoe	fits or
the love	that	died	or didn't
but	lies	open	
arguably	alive		
(or at least)		aligned	

WHICH WALK 35

with which

"seething, wholehearted life force, upright,
unostentatious plainness"
—HILMA AF KLINT, *Notes and Methods*

I collect myself
to regain paradise

recollecting when once

as *Andromeda at the Sea*
to have won a prize

in Af Klint's talented
early life before she

       morphed into a divine
       elasticity of mind realized
       with her circle of women

called The Five or
the Friday Group

delineating the Venusian day's
Venusian way of making

visible abstraction's

      symmetric   state   of vividly

hued   patterns   whose

    obtuse   angles   provide

proofs of desire
and satisfaction,

as of a game with opponents,
companions, judges, fans, flames

all inside what love's mind shows
to be damned as the witches we know

      we are as fallen, flown and
      performatively cloven we

plain say, plain do, and be the lovers and
covens of each one and each other who

    chosen   conjured   overlooked

      underrated   and overloaded

conceive their triumph as that which

      comes from love's mind
      out of love's mouth entirely
      in love's sweet time

against whatever prevents
the gestures and perspectives

necessarily present among
the celebrants of this fraught

place of witching, bitching,
fleeing, and finding

we make as we survive—
we play ourselves being alive

WHICH WALK 36

what it takes

"I was a witch, Lance"
—JACK SPICER, *The Holy Grail*

claiming this
chance chalice

offering the cup
left handedly

to catch the essence of
domestic craft, self-

taught, self-contained,
self-defined and defended

as if the grail as
embodied thought was

Waite's	card's	cloud's	
	crossed	curse	on Spicer's
book's		lover	

as yet another
damsel is offered

brash as she was clear, Claire (Falkenstein), loud, proud, consistently laid
out what was there to be laid, including the permanent wave

of a fabulous fountain
now removed

shaped by the usual
transubstantiation of money

to blood to wine and back
clear as glass, drunk

with disenchantment's
requisite capture of a

goal   achieved   or climax

          aloud   among us   whose

self-same quest zest sought
action's containment

and infusion of facts
lasting into blood drenched

factions of resistance
and shows of force

as people of the cup
collapsed into being

caught in the same place
at the same time as

monsters undermining
the belief in routine

survival in what
it turns out is not

a safe ground from
which to flee or fly

because what is ending
is sending to find

this life or that
story seems

to abide
but does not

making it impossible
to swallow

what was wine then
but is not now

and this is the crux

that the nothing
between us

is what it took
what it takes

walking away to know
to let it go

WHICH WALK 37

permanent wave

"felt structure ... never ending screen"
—CLAIRE FALKENSTEIN

whose goblet practice
is revealed when

what was read
was poured

into the cupped
minds of the ancient

warriors' head cult's
other transformed into

latticed copper and
stained glass locked

in patterned   tresses   dyed

    ironed   dried   and curled

as of the familial
cosmetology whose

arrangements
of heads and

brains I have
counterintuitively

realigned through
the strange fact

of going back
while falling forward

lined like my face ashen
like my hair becoming

pale, plaited, long,
silvered, glassy

catching the sun
done up into

tails   buns   twists

        teased   tangled   waves

pinned in place
that desire

complicated by
passion whose

well-known hand
-held action is both

the cup's destruction
and its infinite display

WHICH WALK 38

back into love

"There is an easy Grail"
—Jack Spicer, *The Holy Grail*

as a hidden dove's
stick nest or steel tower's

lake bound lady seen as
harlot scold's sassy castle or

ruby glass lass in her red robe
unfastened by what drunk

wizard's long night's
unrevealed thousand years

can't not have occurred
though denied and forgotten

as if arithmetic pictured
as a woman wasn't

there then though was

crowned   craved   carved

              saved   moved on   or out

presently circling
the zero which

meant nothing if
not empathy for

a fully composed
mental entity

around which revolving
we/she resolves to see,

      sing   sign   be

            knowing   to go

on this fool's errand
whose map extends

the system of directions
home—as blood flown

from a long dead head

is the quantum explanation
of the grail when just such

a shuck or tale of missed
information with no context

or contact arrives without
completing the feats

pictured as if feet on the
ground of this paradise

of cups and pots caught
by silver chains pouring

water over pale green
flames as if chance

was the change which
proved nothing but that

staying the same is
the diagram of what

happens when the quest ends
with yet another grail ship's

deck graced with
the deadly damsel

              cut   shuffled   stuck

        struck   sucked   under

the grail sea with
what remains

of the fool's plan
to play the hand

the damsel's of nothing

WHICH WALK 39

robe chant imagining

FOR NICK ROBINSON

the robe as clothes
open each which

way allowing what
flows to be the same

as going and sewing—
knowing in advance

to wake each day
again without

expectations great, small
or otherwise played out

like a field,
garden, or feeling

from which floating
forward fast from

minding or not
wrapped in

the visible cloak
of invisible thought

wrought into
waking up

and out
saying while

staying still
finding what

saves everything
and one every-

where for all
the time left

while busy
living, dying,

trying   to sit   still

        quietly   expressed

as being the same
vest dressed in

breath present
while walking,

sitting, lying down,
rising up

WHICH WALK 40

follow the work

". . . very slowly and take each step of the way"
—STANLEY WHITNEY, interview

whose apparent
trajectory when

lines appear
as facts stacked

in the foreground
and back when

loose but determined
actions suggest

what   space   squared   gets

        drawn   into   gesture

a step away
as the exact

color persists us
into existence

which, meant as
event's interrogation,

is the act of moving
across the world

of the square where
freedom's hallucinated

limits spilling over
an imaginary edge

maintain a sure-
handed bespoke

approach   tone   sounded

            out   like   what

is present where

"I could put color next to color
and not lose the air"

WHICH WALK 41

the air

through which its
hard to fly these days

finds me spread
instead across the page

wanting by making
marks to go but also

stay   to walk   groundedly   upright

          finding   what   can't

not be a place or
state of mind whose

invented version of the
day extends outward into

the obvious trap's mapped
maze of ideas masquerading

as luck or love
soaring above

the vicissitudes noted
by everyone to matter

more than whatever
else does

WHICH WALK 42

"NO CLEAN BREAKS"
—CARLOS VILLA, *Itching to Split*

a phrase taken
to heart by mind

(mine) of my
first art teacher for

whom I, barely
existing, scribbled

and was advised
to continue

in art but
didn't until

a half century
down the line(s)

I realized
what was

impossible then
is required now

finding the way
to a surface

including skin
of this freshly drawn

composition of ourselves
with each other

put in place whose
likeness frames

blood, metal, and mirrors,
shattered with matter

stuck and scattered

as fragments from
streets, straightened

     caught   crossed   cast

         hung   and   sung

as the "love/think" continuum
of steel, paste, aluminum,

     faceted   glass   and drafts

        of feathers   facts

cloaks and traps
whose legend

"to learn to fuck yourself
before you can fuck anyone else"

relies on collision,
revision, revival,

and survival to get
beyond death,

as he did, with that
show or this book

The old woman is older still. She notices time collapsing around her, but doesn't care. She makes lines in the shape of her head. She stares into her mirrored eyes, still brown, unlike her haystack hair. Her smile turns into an ache she can't quite get. She carves herself up. Prints a version in reverse. Writing, she thinks, doesn't produce the same immediacy as these face-shaped compositions with their series of takes. The lines reveal what is true of the present as well as the unspoken condition known as later. Her walking satisfies her longing to get to that next place. The lines produced by this movement are the same as her fate. Her face.

WHICH WALK 43

blended pleasure

of ending structured
but reluctant as if an

ace in hand could be
taken to declaim

this catastrophe or that
contagion emblematic

of the age we are in
or I am at, unmasked,

incomplete as thought
which is nevertheless

a sentence stating what
can't be said but

shouted only as
eternity settles in

eyes empty and
mouth open

to replace the face
with what, fixed in

place   is remarked   remasked

          restated   dismounted   scorned

and not quite mourned
as not dead yet but

showing the sequence
to be kept in line

by those left to apprehend
in retrospect

what already
was the end

WHICH WALK 44

articulated lair

"My work has to do with the testing of authority . . .the god that failed."
LOUISE BOURGEOIS, diary notes

where a woman bent
into work stands

hair streaming over
butt and back, knee

up, leaning into
a new genre

whose action
faces out when

memory distends
ending as damage

played, dispelled, arrayed as
uncontained, but uncontested as

"The . . . lairs oscillate on their bases and are weighted in such a way
that if they are pushed they rock and eventually come to rest through
their own stability."

which with facility
not poured but grown

whose chance repetition
thrown again against

the odds being
not even

close to safe but
existing to be

done in with each
gesture poised

to claim a fresh
perspective

that what is made
bereft and betrayed

is impenetrable though
penetrated early

and often by
physical language

        slow   rough   sudden

    depth   debt   finally

found to represent
woman as house

which self-constructs,
conspiring, spider-like,

to be a living
and lived knowledge

whose texted
sketchy world

is sacred, fatal,
and next

WHICH WALK 45

heart left alive

"Only One Sky,"
—TYSHAWN SOREY, *Koan*

in post grail time
adorned by form

which overcomes an over-
armed nation's agenda

of violent past and
future crimes of

      capture   trespass   fear

attack   crusade   dismissal

and assassination

framed as gain while
what remains are

piles of grails drifting
grail upon grail

as not existing but
persistent objects

unconnected to longed for
"Correct Truth" which

crossed descends
into mounds of bloody

children and only
too imaginable danger,

despair, and preoccupation
heady with its heated

bleak   metal   of malleable

          mind   mined

to be aimed
at the strange gains

of ill-gotten power's
pure prevarication's

rapacious waves of false

and desperate beliefs
of slaughter with its

heads on plates and
places inundated

with wasted lives
shaped into lies

of winners, losers,
victims, and systems

—134

not an event but a situation
gunned down, riven, driven

as when grail as face
or flower is erased

by time or when errors
of transcription conflate

the wrong line's right
angle's fallen angel into

the fairy witch continuum
of women tending

their crafted cauldron
filled with split

heads, old newts,
balls, and bones whose

gridded   grotto's   grief

        belief   desacralized

into false castles
of more lies is fastened

with wire clamped
to the battery of any

fly by night
heart left alive

whose graillessness
reconfigured into

a platter or dish
is the host's host

of loaded issues bound
to hold up and on

as this resistance puts
itself into this old one

or that youth whose fear

is the forest of "I am not
Guinevere" but was then

whose "Lady of the Lake
I hate you" claim made

when we saw through time
together was surrounded

by ramparts of thought
constructed by the same

perpetrators true to their
fake tales of grailish

adventures from which
"Awakening" we remain

alert, alive, unfailingly
resilient, and resistant

beneath our
one and only sky

epilogue

The old woman tries to shed her ancient selves but, like the jackets and scarves tied around her waist as she walks, they adhere. She runs hot and is often semi-clothed when her friends are swathed in sweaters. Back in the day she was unafraid of being naked at art events, nude beaches, and other places where it was required. She is still that way, drawing herself, tits out, window shades demurely drawn.

Spying a flock of goldfinches, the woman incorporates them into her project. But she forgets to fly, occupy space, make the way. When she remembers (is remembered) she takes off. Stars appear, a grid, a stand of palms, a crossroads, a short cut down stone steps. The wind comes up, whirling around like the map in her head. When a storm disarranges the neighborhood, she goes out into it. Is probably there now, remembering her lines. Common knowledge. Time of day. The stars are always correct.

ACKNOWLEDGMENTS

Poems from this collection have appeared, sometimes in earlier versions, in *Elderly* (eds. Jamie Townsend & Nicholas DeBoer), *Hambone* (ed. Nathaniel Mackey), and *Posit* (ed. Susan Lewis). My thanks to the editors.

LAURA MORIARTY grew up in Cape Cod and northern California. She studied at Sacramento State University and the University of California at Berkeley. She is the author of numerous collections of poetry and two novels. She recently began a visual art practice, having her second show at Right Window gallery in San Francisco in April of 2025. Moriarty served as Archives Director for the Poetry Center and American Poetry Archives at San Francisco State University. She was Deputy Director of Small Press Distribution for two decades. She has taught at Naropa University, the Otis Art Institute, and Mills College. Her honors include a Poetry Center Book Award, a Wallace Alexander Gerbode Foundation Award in Poetry, a New Langton Arts Award, and a Fund for Poetry grant. She lives in Northern California.

NIGHTBOAT BOOKS

Nightboat Books, a nonprofit organization, seeks to develop audiences for writers whose work resists convention and transcends boundaries. We publish books rich with poignancy, intelligence, and risk. Please visit nightboat.org to learn about our titles and how you can support our future publications.

The following individuals have supported the publication of this book. We thank them for their generosity and commitment to the mission of Nightboat Books:

Kazim Ali • Anonymous (4) • Ava Aviva Avnisan • Jean C. Ballantyne • Will Blythe • V. Shannon Clyne • Theodore Cornwell • Ulla Dydo Charitable Fund • Gisela Gamper • Photios Giovanis • Amanda Greenberger • David Groff • Parag Rajendra Khandhar • Katy Lederer • Shari Leinwand • Elizabeth Madans • Ricardo Maldonado • Ethan Mitchell • Caren Motika • Elizabeth Motika • Asker Saeed • The Leslie Scalapino - O Books Fund • Amy Scholder • Thomas Shardlow • Benjamin Taylor • Jerrie Whitfield & Richard Motika • Clay Williams

This book is made possible, in part, by grants from the National Endowment for the Arts, New York City Department of Cultural Affairs in partnership with the City Council, the New York State Council on the Arts Literature Program, and the Topanga Fund, which is dedicated to promoting the arts and literature of California.